Sports Superstars

David Ortiz

Baseball Star

Mary Ann Hoffman

PowerKiDS press.

New York

Published in 2007 by The Rosen Publishing Group, Inc.
29 East 21st Street, New York, NY 10010

Book Design: Daniel Hosek

Photo Credits: Cover, p. 11 © Otto Greule Jr./Getty Images; p. 5 © Al Bello/Getty Images; p. 7 © Jamie Squire/Getty Images; p. 9 © Craig Melvin/Allsport; p. 13 © Donald Miralle/ Getty Images; pp. 15, 17 © Jed Jacobsohn/Getty Images; p. 19 © Jonathan Daniel/ Getty Images; p. 21 © Doug Pensinger/Getty Images.

Library of Congress Cataloging-in-Publication Data

Hoffman, Mary Ann, 1947-
  David Ortiz : baseball star / Mary Ann Hoffman.
      p. cm. — (Sports superstars)
  Includes index.
  ISBN-13: 978-1-4042-3534-5
  ISBN-10: 1-4042-3534-5
  1. Ortiz, David, 1975-—Juvenile literature. 2. Baseball players—Dominican Republic—Biography—Juvenile literature. I. Title. II. Series.
  GV865.O78H63 2006
  796.357092—dc22
  (B)
                                    2006014619

Contents

David Ortiz is a big man and a powerful hitter. He is called Big Papi.

David was born in the Dominican Republic in 1975. He was signed by the Seattle Mariners in 1992.

David played for the Minnesota Twins from 1997 to 2002. He was hurt in 2001 and did not play many games.

David joined the Boston Red Sox in 2003. He is a DH or designated hitter for the Red Sox.

11

David is a left-handed hitter.
It is hard to strike him out.

David is known as a clutch hitter. A clutch hitter can hit the ball when it is most needed.

21

Glossary

designated hitter (DEH-zihg-nay-tuhd HIH-tuhr)
A player who bats in place of the pitcher.

Dominican Republic (duh-MIH-nih-kuhn
rih-PUH-blik) An island country southeast of the
United States.

home run (HOHM RUN) A hit in baseball that
allows the batter to run around all four bases
and score a run.

strike (STRYK) To swing at the ball and not hit it. To
not swing at the ball when you should try to hit

valuable (VAL-yuh-buhl) Important.

World Series (WUHRLD SEER-eez) A number of
games played every year to decide the best
baseball team.

Books and Web Sites

BOOKS:

Gibbons, Gail. *My Baseball Book*. New York: Harper Collins Publishers, 2000.

Savage, Jeff. *David Ortiz*. Minneapolis, MN: Lerner Publishing Group, 2006.

WEB SITES:

Due to the changing nature of Internet links, PowerKids Press has developed an online list of Web sites related to the subject of this book. This site is updated regularly. Please use this link to access the list:

http://www.powerkidslinks.com/spsuper/ortiz/

Index